An Introduction to the iPad 2

Andrew Edney

Bernard Babani (publishing) Ltd

The Grampians

Shepherds Bush Road

London W6 7NF

England

www.babanibooks.com

Please Note

Although every care has been taken with the production of this book to ensure that all information is correct at the time of writing and that any projects, designs, modifications and/or programs, etc, contained herewith, operate in a correct and safe manner and also that any components specified are normally available in Great Britain, the Publishers and Author(s) do not accept responsibility in any way for the failure (including fault in design) of any project, design, modification or program to work correctly or to cause damage to any equipment that it may be connected to or used in conjunction with, or in respect of any other damage or injury that may be so caused, nor do the Publishers accept responsibility in any way for the failure to obtain specified components.

Notice is also given that if equipment that is still under warranty is modified in any way or used or connected with home-built equipment then that warranty may be void.

ISBN 978 0 85934 727 3

© 2011 BERNARD BABANI (publishing) LTD

First Published – September 2011

Printed and bound in Great Britain for Bernard Babani (publishing) Ltd

About this Book

With Apple iPads becoming more popular, and with the release of the iPad 2, more people than ever are using them for different purposes, be that email, reading books, playing games or many other tasks.

If you have never touched an iPad, using one for the first time can be a little confusing on occasions.

This is where this book comes in. It will provide a gentle introduction into the world of the Apple iPad 2, so giving you enough knowledge and confidence to get out there and do so much more with your iPad than you realised possible.

What you will learn about in this book isn't just confined to the iPad 2 – you can use most of the knowledge and also apply it to the original iPad – the notable exception being anything involving the two cameras, including the FaceTime app.

This book is an independent publication and has not been endorsed by Apple Inc.

Acknowledgements

I would like to offer my thanks to my family and friends for their support and assistance during the long months of writing this book. In addition to the people explicitly named below, I would also like to offer my thanks to all the staff at Babani for once again publishing my book.

Primarily, thanks must go to Katy for her support and thanks to Apollo and Starbuck for keeping me calm when I got too stressed out.

I would also like to thank Caroline Kennedy for her support and assistance – even though she says she isn't "technical" she really helped out a lot – especially now that she has her own iPad!

To anyone I might have missed, a heartfelt thank you goes out to all of you for making this possible. It's been a pleasure.

Trademarks

Apple, iPad, iPad 2, iTunes and FaceTime are either registered trademarks or trademarks of Apple Inc.

All other brand names and product names used in this book are recognised as trademarks, or registered trademarks of their respective companies.

About the Author

ANDREW EDNEY has been an IT professional for more than 15 years and has over the course of his career worked for a range of high-tech companies, such as Microsoft, Hewlett-Packard and Fujitsu Services. He has a wide range of experience in virtually all aspects of Microsoft's computing solutions, having designed and architected large enterprise solutions for government and private-sector customers. Over the years, Andrew has made a number of guest appearances at major industry events, presenting on a wide range of information systems subjects, such as an appearance at the annual Microsoft Exchange Conference in Nice where he addressed the Microsoft technical community on mobility computing. Andrew is currently involved in numerous Microsoft beta programs, including next-generation Windows operating systems and next-generation Microsoft Office products. He actively participates in all Windows Media Center beta programs and was, and still is heavily involved in the Windows Home Server beta program.

Andrew is a Microsoft MVP for Windows Home Server.

Andrew also has a number of qualifications, including an MSc in Network Technologies and Management, he is an MCSE and has numerous MCPs. He is also a Certified Information Systems Security Professional (CISSP) and a Certified Ethical Hacker.

In addition, Andrew has written a number of books on topics such as Windows Home Server, Windows Media Center, Live Communications Server, PowerPoint 2007, networks, Windows Vista, and the Xbox 360. These include *The Windows Home Server User's Guide* (Apress, 2007), *Pro LCS: Live Communications Server Administration* (Apress, 2007), *Getting More from Your Microsoft Xbox 360* (Bernard Babani, 2006), *How to Set Up Your Home or Small Business Network* (Bernard Babani, 2006), *Using Microsoft Windows XP Media Center 2005* (Bernard Babani, 2006), *Windows Vista: An Ultimate Guide* (Bernard Babani, 2007), *PowerPoint 2007 in Easy Steps* (Computer Step, 2007), *Windows Vista Media Center in Easy Steps* (Computer Step, 2007), *Using Ubuntu Linux* (Bernard Babani, 2007), *PowerPoint 2010 in Easy Steps* (In Easy Steps, 2010), *Netbooks in Easy Steps* (In Easy Steps, 2010), *Windows 7 Tweaks Tips and Tricks* (Bernard Babani, 2010), *An Introduction to the MacBook* (Bernard Babani, 2011) and *Working With Windows Small Business Server 2011 Essentials* (MS Press).

Andrew also runs his own IT consulting company, Firebird Consulting, and has a website dedicated to Windows Home Server and the Connected Digital Home, which can be found at http://usingwindowshomeserver.com.

Andrew lives in Wiltshire with his partner, Katy, and their two cats and is the proud owner of an iPad 2.

Contents

Conventions

Throughout this book, you will see a number of information boxes, bounded with either a red line like this…

DESIGNATING A WARNING

…or indeed, a blue line, like this…

DESIGNATING A NOTE, POINT OF INTEREST OR USEFUL TIP

Procedures and walkthroughs are shown as numerical lists, like this:

1. Step 1
2. Step 2

URL's are shown as follows:

http://usingwindowshomeserver.com.

1

Introducing the iPad 2

First off, let me just say congratulations on buying the Apple iPad 2. It is a fantastic device and you should get a lot of enjoyment out of it. Oh, and thank you for buying this book, which will hopefully show you how to use your iPad 2 to get more out of it than you knew were possible.

As you might expect, the iPad 2 is the second iteration of the iPad from Apple. The first one, called the iPad (and now sometimes referred to as the iPad 1) was launched in early 2010 and was a huge success. The iPad 2 was announced in March 2011 and launched shortly afterwards.

Different Versions of the iPad 2

There are two different models of the iPad 2 – the Wi-Fi model and the 3G model. For each of those two models there are three available storage options – 16GB, 32GB and finally 64GB. And then you can choose between a black one or a white one. So, that makes a total of 12 possible choices if you haven't yet purchased yours.

To try to help you narrow down your choices, you might want to consider the following questions:

- Do I want to connect to the Internet from anywhere, whether I am at home, or on the train? If the answer is yes, then you will want to look at the 3G iPad 2. If the answer is no, then the Wi-Fi model should suffice.

- Will I be storing lots of content on my iPad, such as videos and music? If the answer is yes, you should consider either the 32GB or the 64GB version. The 16GB version will suffice for a small amount of content, depending on what that content is, but given the small price difference between the 16GB and the 32GB, I would recommend going for the 32GB to make sure that you have as much space as possible for your money.

A Closer Look at the iPad 2

Let's take a closer look at the iPad 2.

The front, as shown in Figure 1-1, has two elements (along with the actual screen):

A - The Home button

B - The 640 x 480 camera

Figure 1-1 The Front of the iPad 2

The rear, as shown in Figure 1-2, has the most elements:

C – The headphone socket

D – On / off / sleep / wake button

E – The 720p HD camera

F – Mute button / Screen rotation lock

G – Volume control

H – The Dock connector

I – The speaker

Figure 1-2 The Rear of the iPad 2

Charging the iPad

Like any electronic device, the iPad 2 needs power. An average charge for the iPad 2 lasts around 10 hours. Now depending on what you are doing and what you have enabled (Wi-fi and Bluetooth both use up more power) this might be a bit less, but that's still a lot of time on a single charge.

The battery meter is displayed in the top right corner of the screen as a percentage, and if you are getting low on power an image of a battery, in red, will be displayed on the screen to warn you that it's time to charge.

To charge your iPad 2, just connect the USB cable to the iPad via the Dock connector and then connect the other end to the power adaptor and plug that into a power socket. You can see the status of the charge on the screen, as shown in Figure 1-3.

Figure 1-3 Charging the iPad

> You should be able to charge your iPad via the USB port on your computer, but some USB ports, especially on older computers, don't provide enough power to charge the iPad. Check that your laptop will charge the iPad before you leave home without the charger!

iPad 2 vs iPad 1

Some people were disappointed with the iPad 2 not being a huge improvement over the iPad 1. Personally, I thought there were good improvements but maybe Apple could have done more.

The following is a list of improvements over the iPad 1:

- 1GHz Apple A5 processor (instead of an A4)

- Weight is now between 601g and 613g (down from 680g and 730g)

- It's slimmer at 241.2 x 185.7 x 8.8mm (the iPad 1 was 241.2 x 185.7 x 13mm)

- There is a 640 x 480 front camera and a 720p HD rear camera (the iPad 1 didn't have any cameras)

- There is both a black and a white version (instead of just a black one)

> While this book is aimed at using the iPad 2 – the majority of the content is still applicable to the iPad 1 (with the obvious exception of anything involving either the front or rear camera, as the iPad 1 doesn't have this facility).

Accessories for your iPad

There are a number of different accessories you can buy for your iPad. These accessories range from the "must have" – which includes a case or a sleeve to provide protection for the iPad from scratches and other damage - to the "nice to have", which includes stands, car mounts, keyboards, pointing devices and so much more. In fact, there are so many to choose from you might get a little overwhelmed!

Let's just look at the cases. After having spent a lot of money on your iPad 2, the last thing you want to have happen is for it to be scratched or damaged. You would be surprised just how easy it actually is to do that, especially if you carry it in a bag or briefcase.

There are simple cases that just fit around your iPad 2, then there are cases that provide other functions, such as Apple's Smart Covers that not only provides protection for the screen, but automatically powers the iPad on and off when used, and also act as a stand.

Have a long hard think about what you want, because some of these cases and sleeves can cost as much as a quarter of the cost of your iPad!

> If you only buy one accessory, make sure it is some sort of case or sleeve, and buy it as soon as possible. Trust me, you will thank me the first time you drop it or you knock it against something!

Depending on what you are planning to do you with your iPad 2, it might be worth buying a pointing device. These often look like pens with a special tip on the end for using to tap the screen. These will leave less smearing on the screen (as you won't be leaving fingerprint oil), will cause you less strain on your finger and hand, and can also be more precise, especially when playing games. Just make sure you use the right "pen"!

Summary

In this chapter you learnt about the different models and variants of the new iPad 2. You also learnt what each of the buttons and elements on the iPad 2 were, and about some of the different accessories you can get.

2

Switching On Your iPad 2 for the First Time

So you have your charged iPad 2 in your hands and you actually want to start using it. I don't blame you, so let's go through what you need to do in order to actually use it!

When you first press the power button, you will see an image on the screen, like the one in Figure 2-1.

Figure 2-1 Connecting your iPad to iTunes

What this means is that you need to connect your iPad to iTunes on your PC or Mac in order to continue and perform the initial configuration.

This is currently the only way to configure your new iPad so you can't skip this unfortunately.

Getting iTunes for your PC or Mac

As iTunes is a required component of the initial configuration of your iPad 2, you need to have it installed on your PC or Mac. If you have already got iTunes installed then you can skip this section and move on to the next one.

If you have already got iTunes installed, you may need to upgrade it to the latest version in order to use your iPad 2. Just open iTunes and check for an update – if there is one, install it before you continue on with the configuration.

If you haven't got iTunes installed, then you need to follow these steps to download and install it:

1. On the computer that you want to install iTunes on, open a web browser and go to http://www.apple.com/itunes.

2. Click on the Download iTunes button on the webpage.

3. Type in your email address and select your location, as shown in Figure 2-2. Decide if you want to receive update emails from Apple by checking or unchecking the relevant boxes and then click on the Download Now button to download the latest version of iTunes.

Figure 2-2 Downloading iTunes

4. Once iTunes has downloaded, run the downloaded file and follow the instructions to install iTunes. Once the installation has completed you can delete the downloaded file to conserve disc space on your computer.

Configuring the iPad 2 in iTunes

So now you have iTunes installed and are ready to go. To complete the configuration, do the following:

1. Connect the USB cable to the iPad 2, as shown in Figure 2-3 and then connect the other end of the cable to your computer.

2. If iTunes is not already running, it should start automatically, so just wait a few moments until you are prompted.

Figure 2-3 USB cable connected to iPad 2

3. You will be prompted to name your iPad, as shown in Figure 2-4. You can name it anything you want – I called mine Andrew Edney's iPad (because that's what it is!)

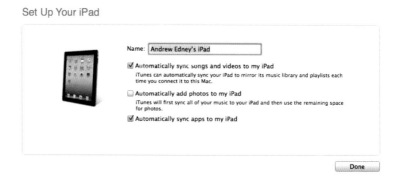

Figure 2-4 Naming your iPad 2

4. You can then choose to automatically sync songs and videos to your iPad (if you already have any in your iTunes library), automatically add photos and

automatically sync apps. Click Done when you are ready to continue.

> We will be covering each of these later in the book, so don't worry too much for now. Personally, I only usually have "Automatically sync apps to my iPad" checked.

Your iPad 2 will now be configured and the selected settings and information will be sync'd to your iPad. If you chose to sync your music, videos and photos then you might have a short wait while it performs this initial sync – so do be patient.

Once the sync has completed, you will be presented with the screen shown in Figure 2-5.

Figure 2-5 Your iPad is now ready to use

5. At this point you can disconnect your iPad 2 from your computer and shut down iTunes.

> We will take a look at using iTunes to do more with your iPad, including the various menu options, later in the book.

Summary

In this chapter you have learnt how to configure your new Apple iPad 2 using iTunes.

3

Using the iPad 2 for the First Time

Now you have performed the initial configuration, you are finally ready to actually start using your iPad 2!

When you first power on the iPad 2, you will see the Home screen showing a number of apps, as shown in Figure 3-1. If you hold your iPad 2 with the Home button facing towards you, the display will appear in portrait mode, if you turn the iPad 2 to the left or right, the display will appear in landscape mode.

You can use your iPad 2 in either landscape mode or portrait mode. The choice is yours and is often made based on what is most comfortable for you. The majority of screenshots in the book are done in landscape mode, primarily because of the format of the book, although that is also my personal preference for normal use as well.

Figure 3-1 The Home screen on the iPad 2

You will notice that there are two areas of the screen. The first, and larger of the two areas contains a number of apps. This number can range from 1 to 20 or more per screen. The second, and smaller of the areas (at the bottom of the screen) is the dock, where there are up to 6 apps (there are 4 by default). The dock is the place you put your most used programs on, because no matter which home screen you are on, the dock is always visible.

By default, the 4 programs are Safari (for surfing the Internet), Mail (for Email), Photos (to view your pictures) and iPod (to listen to music).

But don't worry if these are not the 4 you want on the dock – you can easily change them (and we will cover that in the next chapter).

Launching an Application

Launching an application couldn't be simpler. All you have to do is find the application you want to launch, and just tap on it once.

> If you have more than one screen of applications, you can use your finger and swipe the screen to the left or right, depending on whether there are screens available to the left or right of your current screen.

Closing an Application

When you have finished with an application, or if you want to launch another application as well (after all, your iPad 2 can run more than one application at a time), you just press the Home button.

> When you use the Home button to go back to the home screen, you are not actually closing the application. The application will stay running in the background. This can use valuable system resources and drain your battery power at an increased rate. If you really are sure you have finished with the application, close it properly.

If you want to completely shut down the application:

1. From the home screen, press the Home button twice in quick succession.

2. This will display all the running applications at the bottom of the screen, as shown in Figure 3-2. You will notice that the main desktop is no longer accessible and is faded out. This is called the multitasking tray.

Figure 3-2 The current running applications

3. Tap and hold any of the applications to make them start to "wobble" and for red circles to appear on the top left of each app, as shown in Figure 3-3.

Figure 3-3 Selecting the application to close

4. Press the red circle for each application you want to shut down.

5. When you have shut down all the applications you want, press the Home button twice in quick succession again.

> You can also quickly go to any open application by using the Home button double press and selecting the application you want to go back to – or you can just tap the application again from the home screen, the choice is yours.

Using the Keyboard

As you would have noticed by now, the iPad 2 doesn't have a keyboard, or at least a physical keyboard. Any time that you need to type something a keyboard will appear on the lower part of the screen, as shown in Figure 3-4.

Sometimes the keyboard appears solid, and other times it can appear transparent, depending on the application you are using.

Figure 3-4 The iPad keyboard

To use the keyboard, you just tap the keys. I personally find it a lot easier typing on the iPad when I have the iPad in landscape mode.

There are three different sets of keys on the keyboard. The normal letters appear the first time you use the keyboard. Numbers and some symbols, as shown in Figure 3-5, which can be accessed by tapping the ".?123" button.

Figure 3-5 The iPad keyboard (number display)

And finally more symbols, as shown in Figure 3-6, which are accessed by tapping the "#+=" button on the numbers keyboard.

Figure 3-6 The iPad keyboard (symbol display)

Also, depending on what application you are in, there might be different buttons, such as the Search button replacing the return key.

> You can also use a Bluetooth keyboard with your iPad if you plan on doing a lot of typing.

Cut, Copy and Paste

The ability to cut, copy and paste text or numbers wasn't in the early iOS builds. Thankfully it is there now, and you can use it easily, although it does take a little bit of time to get use to it and to use it correctly.

> You can cut, copy and paste between any application, it doesn't have to be in the same one. For example, you can copy something from an email and paste it into a note.

1. Tap on a word that you want to copy. This will highlight the word, as shown in Figure 3-7.

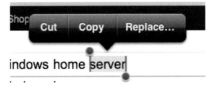

Figure 3-7 Selecting some text

2. Carefully using your finger, drag the start blue line and/or the end blue line to cover all the text you want to select.

3. Tap either the cut or copy button.

4. Go to where you want to paste the text and tap where you want to paste it.

5. Tap the Paste button, as shown in Figure 3-8.

Figure 3-8 Pasting some text

You can also select words, or select everything using Select All, and if you want to replace something with what you are pasting, you just need to highlight it and tap Replace instead of Paste.

Searching

Your iPad 2 comes with a built-in search function.

To search for something, do the following:

1. Swipe your finger to the right until you come to the search screen, as shown in Figure 3-9.

Figure 3-9 The Search screen

2. Tap your search requirements into the search box and then tap the Search button

3. Review the results, as shown in Figure 3-10 and tap on the result that fits what you were looking for.

Figure 3-10 The Search results

Putting the iPad 2 to Sleep

When you have finished using your iPad 2, you can easily put it into sleep mode.

> Your iPad 2 will also go to sleep automatically if it is not used for a set period of time. This is completely configurable and you will learn how to do this later in the book.

To put your iPad 2 to sleep, just press the on/off button once and the screen will go black.

> If you put your iPad 2 to sleep, there is still a small amount of power being used and so your battery will continue to be drained. If you want to conserve the battery as much as possible switch off the iPad 2 instead.

Switching the iPad 2 Off

If you want to switch off your iPad 2, just do the following:

1. Press and hold the on/off button.

2. Slide your finger over the "Slide to power off" button that appears at the top of the screen.

Waking the iPad Up

If you have put your iPad 2 to sleep, it is very easy to wake it up again when you are ready to use it.

Just do the following:

1. Either press the on/off button, or press the Home button.

2. Slide your finger along the "slide to unlock" button that appears at the bottom of the screen, as shown in Figure 3-11.

Figure 3-11 Waking up the iPad

Volume Control and Mute

You can control the volume for any sound coming out of your iPad 2 with the press of a button or a flick of a switch.

To increase or decrease the volume, press the volume button up or down on the side of the iPad 2. A visual representation of the volume will be displayed on screen, as shown in Figure 3-12.

Figure 3-12 Volume level

If you wish to mute, or unmute the volume, flick the mute switch on the side of the iPad 2 (up for unmute, and down for mute), and again a visual representation will be shown on screen, as shown in Figure 3-13.

Figure 3-13 Muting the volume

Locking the Screen Orientation

One of the nice things about the iPad 2 is that you can turn the screen and the orientation changes, so one minute you are using the iPad in portrait, and the next, in landscape.

The problem with this is that sometimes it changes the orientation when you don't want it to, for example if you are not holding it straight or if there is sudden movement. This can be a real pain!

Fortunately there is an easy way of locking the orientation so that it cannot change. In earlier versions of iOS the mute button on the side of the iPad wasn't a mute button at all, it was the screen lock. However an update to the software changed that and people were not happy about it.

Anyway, if you want to set the orientation to lock, or unlock, follow these steps:

1. If you want to lock the orientation, make sure the iPad is orientated in the way you want to lock.

2. Double tap the Home button to launch the multitasking tray.

3. Swipe your finger to the right until the orientation lock button is displayed, as shown in Figure 3-14.

Figure 3-14 The orientation lock button

4. Tap the orientation lock button to lock the orientation in whatever orientation your iPad is in. The button will change to a padlock, as shown in Figure 3-15.

Figure 3-15 Orientation is locked

5. Press the Home button to close the multitasking tray.

6. Repeat the process to unlock the orientation as required.

> You can change the side switch on your iPad to set the lock rotation instead of muting the volume. You can do this via the Settings app.

Summary

In this chapter you have learnt all about using the iPad 2 for the first time. This included learning about launching and shutting down applications, how to use the keyboard, and more.

Keep reading though, there is more to come, including how to personalise the iPad 2 and how to use all the features.

4

Personalising Your Experience

You could probably happily use your iPad 2 just as it is, but where would the fun be in that? After all, you can personalise the look of your iPad, so why don't you?

There are a number of different elements you can personalise, including the position of the application icons, the desktop wallpaper, the lock screen wallpaper, sounds and even adding a passcode to keep your iPad secure.

Moving Apps Around

Whenever you add an app, it will appear in an available space on the home screen. Sometimes you won't want it where it gets placed, and so you can move it.

To move an app, do the following:

1. Tap and hold any app until all the apps start to wobble.

2. Tap and hold a specific app and move it to a new position on the screen, or if you want to move it to

another screen just drag it all the way to the left or right until the screen changes.

3. Press the Home button when you have moved all the apps you want.

> If you move an app to the right and there isn't a new home screen available, one will be created for you automatically. You don't need to fill up a screen before moving on to the next one.

Using Folders

As you will soon notice if you add lots of apps to your iPad, the home screens become full and you may spend a few moments searching through the screens to find what you are looking for.

This is what Folders are for – you can create a folder and it can hold a number of apps. For example, let's say you wanted to put all your games in a folder, now you can have them all in one place and it only takes up one space on the home screen.

To create a folder, do the following:

1. Tap and hold an app you want to move into a folder – the apps will all start to wobble.

2. Drag the app and drop it on top of another app that you also want in the folder.

3. The folder will automatically be created with those two apps in, and you can type in a name for that folder, as shown in Figure 4-1.

4. Press the Home button or tap any part of the screen to finish.

5. Drag any other apps you want to include in the folder and drop them in there.

> The iPad is quite smart at times – if you move some apps into a folder that are camera related, such as those in the example, the iPad automatically names the folder, in this case to Photography.

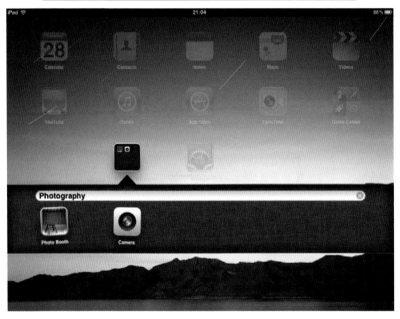

Figure 4-1 Adding apps to a folder

You will then see the folder displayed on the home page, as shown in Figure 4-2.

Figure 4-2 The new folder

All you have to do then is tap on the folder to reveal the apps inside.

To move an app back to the home screen, do the following:

1. Tap on the folder to open it and display the apps held within it, as shown in Figure 4-3.

Figure 4-3 The apps in the folder

2. Tap and hold any of the apps until they start to wobble.

3. Drag the app you want to move back to the home screen and let go.

4. Repeat as necessary.

When the last app has been removed from the folder, the folder itself will disappear so you don't need to worry about deleting the folder if you don't want it any more.

Changing the Wallpaper

Another great way to personalise your iPad 2 is to use your own pictures as wallpaper. There are two different places you can have your own wallpaper – the Home screen and the Lock screen.

If order to use a picture as wallpaper you must have that picture stored on the iPad. If you haven't got any pictures on the iPad you can copy some pictures to it using iTunes. To learn how to do this, see later in the book.

There are two different ways of selecting and setting the wallpaper – either using the Settings options or by selecting a picture within the Photos app.

I find it easier to select pictures from the Photos app as they are easier to see all in one place, but the choice is yours.

To use your pictures as wallpaper from the Photos app, do the following:

1. Find the Photos app and tap it.

2. From the available photos, as shown in Figure 4-4, tap on the picture you want to use.

Figure 4-4 Available pictures on your iPad

3. Tap the button in the top right corner, as shown in Figure 4-5.

Figure 4-5 Options button

4. Tap the "Use as Wallpaper" button, as shown in Figure 4-6.

Figure 4-6 Use as wallpaper

5. You can then tap either "Set Lock Screen", "Set Home Screen" or "Set Both", as shown in Figure 4-7.

Figure 4-7 Selecting which screen

Figure 4-8 shows the new Home screen.

Figure 4-8 The new Home Screen

> You can use the same picture for both the Home Screen and the Lock Screen if you want – but where's the fun in that?

To use your pictures as wallpaper from the Settings app, do the following:

1. Find the Settings app and tap it.

2. Tap Brightness & Wallpaper from the Settings column, as shown in Figure 4-9.

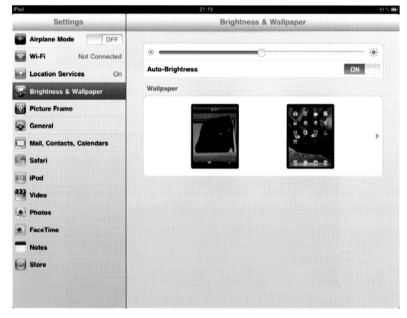

Figure 4-9 Changing the wallpaper in Settings

3. Tap the left image for the Lock screen and the right image for the Home screen.

4. Tap the library you want to search through for your pictures, as shown in Figure 4-10.

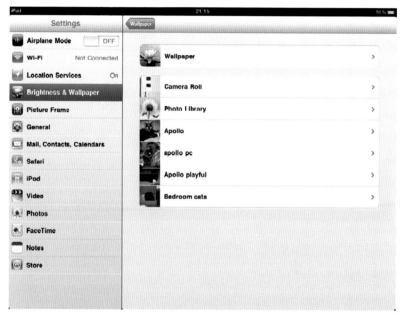

Figure 4-10 Selecting which folder to view

5. Tap on the picture you want to use.

6. You can then tap either "Set Lock Screen", "Set Home Screen" or "Set Both".

Figure 4-11 shows the new Lock screen.

Figure 4-11 The new Lock Screen

Sounds

Certain events on your iPad 2 have sounds associated with them, for example sending and receiving email and even keyboard clicks.

You can choose whether to have these sounds on or off.

To see these settings and make changes, do the following:

1. Tap on the Settings app.

2. From the Settings list, tap on General.

3. Tap on Sounds.

4. Raise or lower the volume using the slider, as shown in Figure 4-12. You can also choose to switch OFF or ON various options.

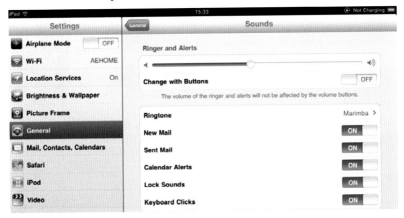

Figure 4-12 Sounds options

You may have noticed an option called Ringtone. Your first thought might be "why is there a ringtone option"? After all, it's an iPad, not an iPhone. Well, this option is for use with the FaceTime application.

> For more information on FaceTime, see later in the book.

1. From the Sounds option, tap on Ringtone.

2. Choose a new ringtone from the list, as shown in Figure 4-13. When you tap on one you will be played a sample of the sound.

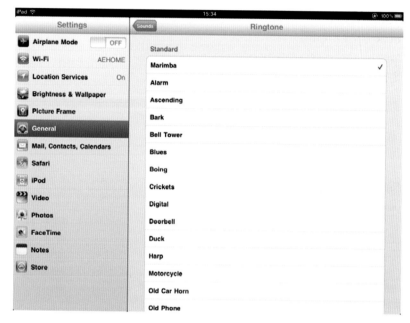

Figure 4-13 Choosing your ringtone

Even if you have the iPad set to mute, you will still hear the sample sound, so be careful not to annoy people around you if you want to test every single sample!

Securing your iPad 2

If like me you are security conscious, then you will probably want to secure your iPad 2 with a Passcode. This will stop people from just picking it up and using it if you leave it lying around. When you try to use the iPad 2, you are asked to enter your passcode, as shown in Figure 4-14. No passcode, no access – simple!

Figure 4-14 Enter your passcode

If you are going to set a passcode, one of the things you need to decide on is the amount of time before the iPad auto-locks, that is, how long until it locks when you are not using it?

To check and change the auto-lock time:

1. Tap on the Settings app.

2. Tap on General from the Settings list.

3. Tap on Auto-Lock.

4. Tap on the time you want to set for the auto-lock, as shown in Figure 4-15.

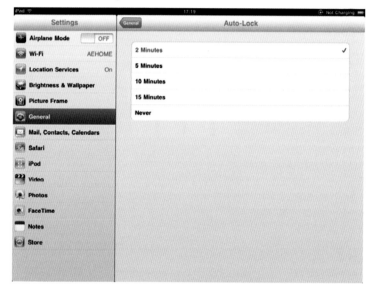

Figure 4-15 Selecting an auto-lock frequency

Don't select Never if you want to use a passcode unless you remember to manually lock your iPad every single time you leave it.

Now that has been done, it is time to set the passcode.

To set the passcode, do the following:

1. Tap on General to display the list of options again.

2. Tap on Passcode Lock.

3. Tap on Turn Passcode On, as shown in Figure 4-16.

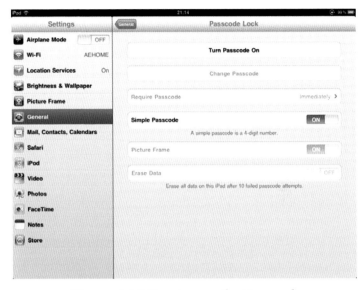

Figure 4-16 Turning on the Passcode

4. Enter 4 numbers that you want to use as your passcode, as shown in Figure 4-17.

Figure 4-17 Choosing a Passcode

5. Enter the 4 numbers again to confirm the passcode.

If you want to change your passcode at any time, you can:

1. From the Passcode Lock screen, tap Change Passcode.

2. Enter your old passcode.

3. Enter your new passcode twice.

The 4-digit number you are using for your passcode is referred to as "simple". If you feel you need to use something more secure than 4 numbers you can by doing the following:

1. From the Passcode Lock screen, slide the Simple Passcode button from ON to OFF.

2. Enter your old passcode.

3. Now type in a new passcode, as shown in Figure 4-18. This can be a word, a number, a phrase, anything you like. Tap return or Next to continue.

> Whatever you do, do not forget the passcode because without it you will not be able to use your iPad and you will have to perform a reset.

Figure 4-18 Entering a new complex passcode

4. Re-enter the new passcode.

Now if you are REALLY security conscious, you can have your iPad erase all your data after 10 failed attempts with the passcode.

Should you choose to use this extreme setting, do the following:

1. From the Passcode Lock screen, slide the Erase Data button from OFF to ON.

2. You will need to confirm you understand the implication of this setting, as shown in Figure 4-19, by tapping Enable.

Figure 4-19 Enabling Erase Data

To turn off the Passcode Lock at any time, just do the following:

1. From the Passcode Lock screen, tap Turn Passcode Off.

2. Enter your passcode.

Brightness

Depending on your surroundings, you might find that your iPad 2 screen is either too bright, or not bright enough. Don't worry, because like a lot of other things with the iPad, you can change it!

To change the brightness setting:

1. Tap on the Settings app.

2. Tap on Brightness & Wallpaper.

3. Use your finger to slide the brightness bar left or right, as shown in Figure 4-20.

Figure 4-20 Setting the brightness

There is an Auto-Brightness setting, which is ON by default that should detect your surrounding and adjust accordingly, however users have reported mixed results so you may need to manually change the brightness on occasion.

Adding Apps to the Dock

One of the best ways to personalise your experience is to add your most used apps to the dock. This way, no matter what home screen you are in, those apps are always there.

By default there are four apps in the dock already (Safari, Mail, Photos and iPod), and you can have up to six, so make them count.

To add an app to the dock, do the following:

1. Tap and hold any app until they all start to wobble.

2. Tap and hold the app you want to add to the dock and drag it to dock.

3. Repeat until all the apps you want to appear in the dock (up to 6 remember) are there, as shown in Figure 4-21.

Figure 4-21 Filling the dock

4. Press the Home button.

Summary

In this chapter you have learnt how to personalise your iPad 2 to make it more your own. You have also learnt how to use your own pictures as wallpaper, how to move apps to different home screens and how to store them in folders for easier access. In the next chapter you will learn how to connect your iPad 2 to your network.

5

Connecting the iPad 2 to a Network

One of the things you will want to do is connect your iPad 2 to your home network (or any other network for that matter). This will enable you to surf the Internet, check your email, download and update apps, and so on.

> If you don't have the 3G version of the iPad 2, then this will be the only way you can connect to the Internet.

To connect your iPad 2 to a network, perform the following steps:

> Before you start, make sure you have the network name you want to connect to and also the password (assuming there is one).

1. On the iPad 2, locate the Settings app and tap it, as shown in Figure 5-1.

Figure 5-1 Choosing Settings

2. From the left-hand Settings pane, as shown in Figure 5-2, tap Wi-Fi.

Figure 5-2 Selecting Wi-Fi in Settings

3. If Wi-Fi is already switched on, then you can skip to step 4, otherwise slide the Wi-Fi button on the right-hand side from OFF to ON.

4. After a few moments, any available wireless networks will then be displayed, as shown in Figure 5-3. Just tap on the network that you want to connect to.

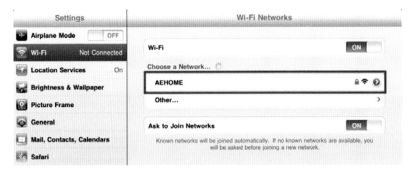

Figure 5-3 Selecting a wireless network

> The padlock symbol indicates that the wireless network is protected, which means you will need a password to connect to it.

5. If the network is protected, you will need to type in the password, as shown in Figure 5-4, and then tap Join.

Figure 5-4 Entering the password

After the connection has been made, you will see the list of networks again, as shown in Figure 5-5, only this time you will see check a mark against the network you are connected to.

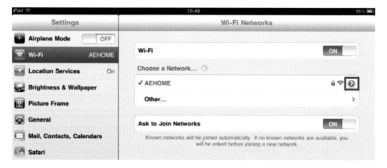

Figure 5-5 Showing the connected network

6. If you want to see specific information about this network, or you want to disconnect from the network, just tap the arrow icon shown in line with the connected network.

As you will see from Figure 5-6, various information about the network is displayed, including the IP address given to your iPad.

To disconnect from the network:

1. Tap the Settings app.

2. Tap Wi-Fi from the list of available settings.

3. Tap the arrow icon shown in line with the connected network you want to disconnect from.

4. Tap the "Forget this Network" button.

Even if you choose to "Forget this Network" you can connect to it again at any time by performing the same steps above.

5. Tap the Forget button that appears.

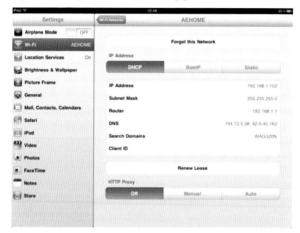

Figure 5-6 Information about the network

Leaving Wi-Fi mode enabled uses the battery at a faster rate, so if you know that you are not going to be connecting to a wireless network you should consider switching it off until the time you need to use it.

Airplane Mode

Airplane Mode is a special setting that turns off Wi-Fi and Bluetooth signals and the Global Positioning System (GPS) reception is also turned off. It is called Airplane Mode as all those features would need to be turned off if you were on a plane.

> You don't just have to use Airplane Mode when you are flying. Airplane Mode also conserves battery power so you might want to consider switching it on if you are not going to use those features for a short time.

To enable Airplane Mode:

1. Tap the Settings app.

2. On the top left of the screen you will see the Airplane Mode switch, as shown in Figure 5-7. Slide the switch to the right to switch it ON.

Figure 5-7 Airplane Mode

You will now see that Airplane Mode is enabled, as shown in Figure 5-8. You will also see that both iPad and the Wireless symbol on the top left of the iPad have been replaced with an image of an airplane.

Figure 5-8 Airplane Mode ON

Checking for the Airplane symbol is a quick way of checking if your iPad 2 has been set to Airplane Mode.

To disable Airplane Mode:

1. Tap the Settings app.

2. On the top left of the screen you will see the Airplane Mode switch, as shown in Figure 5-8. Slide the switch to the left to switch it OFF.

Being Asked to Join Networks

When you have Wi-Fi enabled, if you are not joined to a known network (i.e. a network you have previously joined) every time your iPad finds a new wireless network you will be prompted to join it. This can be a pain, especially if you are travelling or you are in an area with lots of available networks.

Fortunately, this is easy to rectify:

1. Tap on the Settings app.

2. Tap Wi-Fi from the list of available settings.

3. On the right-hand side, locate the "Ask to Join Networks" setting, as shown in Figure 5-9 and slide the button to the left, which will change the setting to OFF.

Figure 5-9 Disabling Ask to Join Networks

You will still be able to find and join wireless networks with this set to OFF, just as you did previously, but know you won't be prompted everytime.

3G

If you have a 3G iPad 2, then you can connect to the Internet using 3G as well as wireless.

> As well as needing the 3G iPad 2 to connect via 3G, you will also need a sim card and data plan from a mobile provider. Be careful when using 3G, if you go over your included monthly data you may end up with a very large phone bill!

These are the steps you need to perform to set up and enable 3G:

1. Tap on the Settings app.

2. Tap on Cellular Data from the left-hand column.

3. If Cellular Data is switched off, slide the button to the right to the ON position.

4. Tap View Account and work your way through the questions.

Summary

In this chapter you learnt about finding and connecting to wireless networks from your iPad 2. You also learnt about Airplane Mode and how to enable 3G access.

6

Doing More With iTunes

iTunes is used for a lot more than just configuring your iPad 2 for the first time. You can use it to update the iPad, backup and restore it, and even search for and buy applications.

Backing Up Your iPad 2

Backing up your iPad 2 is a very good idea. After all, if anything happens to your iPad you wouldn't want to lose all your data would you?

Backing up is very simple and in fact only requires you to connect your iPad 2 to your computer with the USB cable. iTunes will then start and your iPad will be automatically backed up for you – simple as that.

You can see the progress of the backup at the top of the iTunes window, as shown in Figure 6-1.

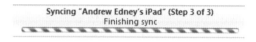

Figure 6-1 Backup status

Restoring Your iPad 2

OK, so what if something goes wrong with your iPad 2? It does happen. Maybe you have an app that has caused a problem? Maybe you just want to recover your last backup?

To restore your iPad 2, do the following:

1. From iTunes, ensure your iPad is selected from the Device list in the left-hand column and click the Restore button, as shown in Figure 6-2.

Figure 6-2 Selecting to perform a restore

2. You will be asked to confirm that you want to perform the restore, as shown in Figure 6-3. Just click Restore to continue.

Figure 6-3 Confirming the restore

Your computer will now contact Apple and check for the latest version of the iOS for your iPad 2, and if necessary will download it for you automatically. When this process is complete you will see a message telling you that your iPad has been restored to factory settings, as shown in Figure 6-4.

Figure 6-4 The restore to factory settings is complete

3. You will then have the option of setting up your iPad as though it was brand new (just like you did originally back in Chapter 2) or restoring it from backup, as shown in Figure 6-5. The latest backup will be selected automatically so you can click Continue if that is the one you want to restore.

Figure 6-5 Choosing whether to restore or not

4. If you want to choose a different backup to restore, click on the backup list to display the available backups, as shown in Figure 6-6. Then just choose the backup to restore and click Continue.

Figure 6-6 Selecting the backup to restore

5. Now just sit back and wait for the restore to complete. When it is done you will see the message shown in Figure 6-7.

Figure 6-7 Restore is complete

Updating Your iPad 2

Apple are always updating the software for the iPad. These updates can be anything from security updates and bug fixes, to introducing new software and features.

> Currently the way Apple do the updates is for you to download a complete image of the new software and apply it to your iPad – so don't be surprised if the update is over 600MB just for a minor change. This is normal and rumour has it will change in a later version.

1. When you connect your iPad 2 to your computer, iTunes automatically checks to see if there is an update available. If there is, you will be informed, as shown in Figure 6-8.You then have the option to Cancel (which ignores the update), Download and Update, or just Download Only. Make your selection by clicking on the one you want.

Figure 6-8 An update is available

> If you don't want to sit there and wait for the download and you want to use your iPad, just click on the Download Only option and then you can apply the update another time.

2. You must then confirm you want to update your iPad, as shown in Figure 6-9.

Figure 6-9 Confirm you want to update

Now just sit back and wait for the update to download and install. Depending on the speed of your Internet connection, this process can take quite a while, especially if it happens to be the same day that Apple have released the update.

> You can always check to see what the update contains to decide whether or not you want to install it, but if the update includes any bug fixes or more importantly, security fixes, you should apply them as soon as possible.

Other iPad Options in iTunes

As well as the Summary tab, there are a number of other tabs that contain a host of other options.

The Info tab, as shown in Figure 6-10, enables you to use MobileMe (which is a paid-for service from Apple) to sync your email, calendars, contacts and more with your iPad. But don't worry, you don't need a subscription to MobileMe to do this.

Figure 6-10 The Info tab

You can also choose to sync various elements with Outlook, or Google, Windows or Yahoo, as shown in Figure 6-11.

Figure 6-11 Sync with different providers

Make any changes you want and click on the Sync button.

The next tab is Apps, as shown in Figure 6-12.

Figure 6-12 The Apps tab

From here you can select which apps to sync (if you also have an iPhone, any apps will be available here as well).

> To learn more about apps, take a look at the App Store chapter later in the book.

You can also move the apps around on the right-hand screen which can often be quicker than moving them around on the iPad itself.

> After making any changes, don't forget to click Apply or the changes will be lost.

The next tab is called Music. From here you can sync any music that you have stored in your music library within iTunes.

The next two tabs are Films and TV Programmes. From here you can sync any movies or TV Shows that you have stored in your library within iTunes.

> You can buy movies and TV shows from iTunes to watch on your iPad. Why not take a look to see what is there by clicking on the iTunes Store link in the left column.

Another tab is Photos. From here you can sync any photos (and even videos) that you have stored in your library within iTunes.

> If you click on "Selected albums…." then you can selects folders of photos that are stored on your computer rather than from iTunes.

When you install certain apps on your iPad, they can add another tab to iTunes, for example, if you install iBooks on your iPad, an iBooks tab will appear in iTunes. This is all designed to make the process of adding and deleting items that little bit easier.

Copying Media Directly to the iPad

There might be some media, for example some music or some pictures that you want to have on your iPad, but you don't want to put in iTunes.

You can do this by ensuring that iTunes is open, your iPad is connected to your computer and then just dragging the items you want copied to your iPad into iTunes and dropping them directly into the DEVICES area in the left-hand column, as shown in Figure 6-13.

Figure 6-13 Devices in iTunes

Not every item of media can be copied to your iPad. If you try to copy something that cannot be played back then iTunes just won't let you do it. If this happens check to see if what you are trying to copy is supported.

Summary

In this chapter you have learnt that iTunes can be used for much more than just the initial configuration of your iPad. For example, you can use it to sync music, photos and even movies and tv shows to your iPad, and also use iTunes to back up.

7

Surfing the Internet

One of the many things that your iPad 2 can enable you to do is to surf the Internet. You can visit websites, bookmark your favouries, search for things and do pretty much everything you would expect to do on the Internet.

> Don't forget that you need to be connected to either a wireless network or via 3G in order to surf the Internet.

The app used for surfing the Internet is called Safari, as shown in Figure 7-1.

Figure 7-1 The Safari App

To start surfing the Internet, do the following:

1. Tap on Safari.

2. Tap on the box at the top of the screen, as shown in Figure 7-2.

Figure 7-2 Typing in a URL

3. Type in the URL (address) of the website that you want to visit and then tap the Go button.

4. The website will then be contacted and loaded just as you would expect and the site displayed for you, as shown in Figure 7-3.

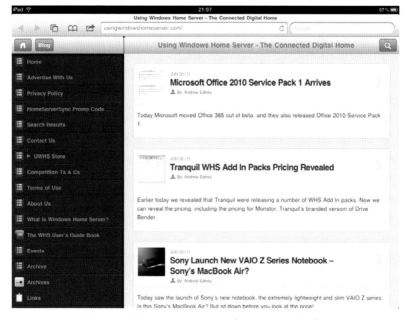

Figure 7-3 Viewing a web page in Safari

Navigating and Using Safari

When you are viewing web pages and sites, you may want to go back, or even go forward once you have gone back to different pages. To do this you just use the arrows on the top bar, as shown in Figure 7-4.

Figure 7-4 Navigating pages

Opening a New Safari Page

You may want to have more than one page open at a time. Unlike a browser in Windows or on the Mac, you can't have multiple instances of Safari running, but what you can have is multiple Safari pages open.

To open a new Safari page, do the following:

1. Tap on the pages icon in the top bar, as shown in Figure 7-5.

Figure 7-5 Opening a new page

2. Tap on the New Page box, as shown in Figure 7-6 to open a new page.

Figure 7-6 Selecting a new page

3. Type in the URL for the new site just as before.

You can easily switch between pages by tapping the pages icon and then tapping on the site you want.

When you have finished with a page, you can easily close it by tapping on the X in the top left corner in the pages view.

Searching the Web

Just like any other browser, you can search for something easily. Obviously you can just visit the URL of your favourite search engine, or you can use the in-built search box within Safari.

To search for something using the search box:

1. Tap on the Google search box, as shown in Figure 7-7.

Figure 7-7 Searching the web

2. Type in whatever it is you want to search for and then tap the Search button on the keyboard.

3. View the displayed results, as shown in Figure 7-8.

Figure 7-8 The search results

4. Tap on any of the results to visit that website.

Changing the Default Search Engine

Currently the default search engine within Safari is Google. If you don't want to use Google as your default you can change it to either Yahoo! or Bing.

To change the default search engine:

1. From the Home screen tap on Settings.

2. From the Settings list, tap on Safari.

3. Tap on Search Engine, as shown in Figure 7-9.

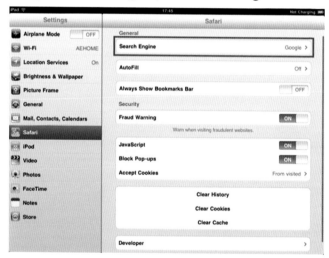

Figure 7-9 Safari Settings

4. Tap on the search engine name you want to use, as shown in Figure 7-10.

Figure 7-10 Selecting your Search Engine

Bookmarks

Bookmarks are used to enable you to quickly pick websites you want to visit from a list, instead of having to type in the complete URL each time.

To view your bookmarks:

1. Tap on the Bookmarks icon, as shown in Figure 7-11.

Figure 7-11 Bookmarks

2. Tap on the site you want to visit from your list of available bookmarks, as shown in Figure 7-12.

Figure 7-12 Your bookmarks

Adding a bookmark is easy as well, just do the following:

1. Visit the site you want to bookmark.

2. Tap on the options icon, as shown in Figure 7-13.

Figure 7-13 Options

3. Tap on Add Bookmark from the available options, as shown in Figure 7-14.

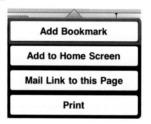

Figure 7-14 Add a bookmark

You can also add a link to a website directly onto your Home screen by tapping on the Add to Home Screen button. This will place the link on the Home screen and all you have to do is tap it to open Safari and visit the website.

If you want to remove a bookmark, just do the following:

1. Tap on the bookmarks icon.

2. Tap Edit.

3. Tap the red circle against the bookmark, as shown in Figure 7-15.

Figure 7-15 Removing a bookmark

4. Tap Delete.

5. Tap Done.

Tidying Up After Yourself

Whenever you visit a website, information is stored on your iPad 2. This will include the site URL in the History file, any cookies that might be pushed from the site and any site information in the cache.

> It is a good idea to periodically clear down this information and tidy up after yourself. It frees up space on your iPad.

To delete some or all of this stored information, do the following:

1. Tap on Settings from the Home screen.

2. Tap on Safari from the Settings list.

3. Tap on the clearing option you want to use, as shown in Figure 7-16.

Clear History
Clear Cookies
Clear Cache

Figure 7-16 Clearing options

4. Confirm your selection by tapping Clear when prompted.

> When you clear one of the settings, that information is gone. But don't worry you can always visit the site again!

Support for Adobe Flash

At this time there is still no support for Adobe's Flash product which means if you visit a website that uses Flash those elements will just appear as either empty boxes or boxes with question marks in.

Summary

In this chapter you have learnt how to surf the Internet using Safari. You also learnt about bookmarks and how to clean up after yourself.

8

Using Email

Your iPad 2 comes with a built-in email client so you can check, read and send emails directly from your iPad without having to use a webmail client. But before you can use the email client you need to configure it to work with your email.

> If you don't have an email account, now is a good time to get one. There are plenty that are free, and the iPad easily supports email accounts from the likes of Google and Yahoo!

Configuring Email

> You will need your email account details (including password) before continuing.

To configure an email account with Mail, do the following:

1. Tap on the Mail app, as shown in Figure 8-1.

Figure 8-1 Mail

2. Tap on the name of your email provider, as shown in Figure 8-2. If your provider is not listed, try tapping Other.

Figure 8-2 Selecting your email provider

3. Enter your account details in each line, as shown in Figure 8-3, then tap Next to continue.

Figure 8-3 Entering your account details

4. Depending on the type of account you are adding you will be asked what features to enable, as shown in Figure 8-4.

Figure 8-4 Enabling features on Gmail

5. Tap Save to finish.

Using Email

Now that you have configured your email account, it is time to start using it.

Figure 8-5 shows the contents of your Inbox. The screen is split between a left-hand column that shows your emails and the right-hand column that shows the content of the email.

Figure 8-5 Your Inbox

To send a new email:

1. Tap on the new email icon, as shown in Figure 8-6.

Figure 8-6 New email icon

2. Type in To:, Subject:, and your Message into the blank email, as shown in Figure 8-7, then tap Send.

Figure 8-7 Typing a new email

To reply to an email:

1. In the email you want to reply to, tap the reply icon, as shown in Figure 8-8.

Figure 8-8 Replying to an email

You can also select Forward instead of reply.

2. Type your reply and tap Send.

To delete an email:

1. From the email you want to delete, tap the delete icon as shown in Figure 8-9.

Figure 8-9 Deleting an email

> Depending on your email account, you may have different icons – for example Gmail doesn't have a delete icon, it has an Archive icon instead. Check with your email provider for more details on what can be done.

Email Settings

There are a number of different settings you can configure, some of which will depend on the type of email account you have, but most are account independent.

To access email settings:

1. Tap on Settings from the Home screen.

2. Tap on Mail, Contacts, Calendars from the Settings list.

From here you can add or remove email accounts, change the amount of messages to show, have a preview of the email message, and much more.

One of the key things to decide is when you want the email messages to appear.

1. Tap on Fetch New Data.

2. You can choose to have Push ON or OFF, as shown in Figure 8-10.

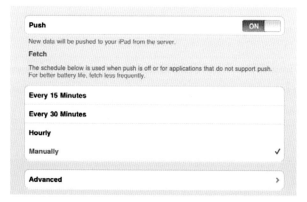

Figure 8-10 Fetch new data settings

Choose your settings carefully as using Push (which will push every new email to your inbox) or having a frequent fetch (which checks email for you and pulls down any new messages) uses more battery and so reduces your available power. The best setting for battery conservation is Push set to OFF and Fetch set to Manually, which means you can just tap the check message button yourself.

Each time you send a new email a signature will appear by default. This signature says "Sent from my iPad" and appears at the end of each email. When you first get your iPad that looks quite cool, but after a while it can get boring, so you may want to change it, or remove it completely.

To make changes to the signature:

1. Scroll through the available settings until you see Signature – tap it.

2. Type in what you want your signature to look like, as show in Figure 8-11.

Figure 8-11 Your signature

3. If you don't want a signature, tap the Clear button. Then either press the Home button or tap on another Settings tab.

You can have more than one email account on your iPad. This can be useful, but at the same time can take a little getting used to. Only one of the email accounts can be the default account. This is the account that unless you manually choose another account, will be used to send email. Most of the time that will be fine, but there might come a time when you want to change it if you start using one account more than the other.

To set your default email account:

1. From the Mail, Contacts, Calendars settings, scroll down until you find Default Account – tap it.

2. Tap on the account you wish to use as your default from the list of added accounts, as shown in Figure 8-12.

Figure 8-12 Choosing your default email account

3. Then either press the Home button or tap on another Settings tab.

Summary

In this chapter you have learnt how to add email accounts and how to use email to send, receive, view and delete your email messages. You have also learnt how to change some of the settings, including changing or removing a signature block.

9 —

The App Store

One of the features of your iPad 2 is the App Store. The App Store provides both paid and free software that you can search for, download and install. This software includes games, music, productivity tools and so much more. It also handles updates to the software and allows you to view reviews and even add your own review if you wish.

> You can also use iTunes on your computer to locate, buy and download items from the App Store. They won't be installed on your iPad until you perform a sync. For more information on this, see later in this chapter.

Launching the App Store

1. Locate and tap on the App Store app to open the App Store, as shown in Figure 9-1.

Figure 9-1 Locating and opening the App Store

2. When the App Store opens, you will be presented with the Featured screen, as shown in Figure 9-2. This screen shows various items, including new and noteworthy apps.

> You will need to be connected to a wireless network in order to view the contents of the App Store from your iPad.

Figure 9-2 Items in the App Store

The Featured screen is broken up into various sections. You can see the New & Noteworthy apps, the App of the Week, you can search the App Store, and even display apps based on popularity and release date.

Searching for and selecting Apps

If you know what app you want, you can either search for it using the Search box, or you can tap through various categories, as shown in Figure 9-3.

Figure 9-3 Categories in the App Store

So let's say that you want an app that you can use for Twitter.
Perform the following steps to locate and download the app:

1. Tap the Search box, and type Twitter then tap Search.

2. The results will be displayed for you, as shown in
   Figure 9-4. As you can see, some of the apps are
   shown as FREE, and some have a cost associated with
   them. The choice is yours, just tap on the one you are
   interested in, or want to find out more about.

Figure 9-4 The Search Results

There are often free and paid versions of the same software available. The free version might contain adverts and be limited in some way. If you are not sure if that is the app you want to buy, trying the free version first can be useful.

3. Information on that app will then be displayed, as shown in Figure 9-5. If you decide that it is the one you want, tap on the Free button or Price button depending on what type of app it is.

Figure 9-5 Information on an app in the App Store

4. Tap on the INSTALL APP button that now replaces the Free or Price button.

5. You will be asked to enter your Apple ID password, as shown in Figure 9-6. Enter your password and tap OK.

Figure 9-6 Sign in with your Apple ID

6. If this is the first time you have used your Apple ID on the iPad you may be asked to verify your account, as shown in Figure 9-7, do so if requested.

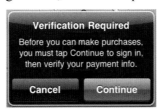

Figure 9-7 Account verification required

7. The app will now be downloaded and installed for you, as shown in Figure 9-8 and then you can then start using it straight away.

Figure 9-8 The app is being installed

Your Purchase History

Every time you download something from the App Store, even if it is a free app, it is recorded in your Purchase History. This can be useful if you think you may have tried an app in the past and can't remember.

If you want to check your purchase history, just tap Purchased from the App Store menu.

You will then be presented with a list of everything you have "purchased" and whether or not it is currently installed, as shown in Figure 9-9.

Figure 9-9 Your Purchase History

To make it easy to see what hasn't been installed on this iPad you can tap on the "Not On This iPad" button and then choose what to install. This is useful if you have more than one iPad or if you have upgraded from an iPad 1.

Updating App Store Purchases

As with the iOS, apps in the App Store also need to be updated from time to time.

To check if there are any available updates, tap on Updates from the App Store menu.

If there are any updates available, they will be displayed and you can choose to update them, or if nothing needs updating you will be told all of your apps are up to date, as shown in Figure 9-10.

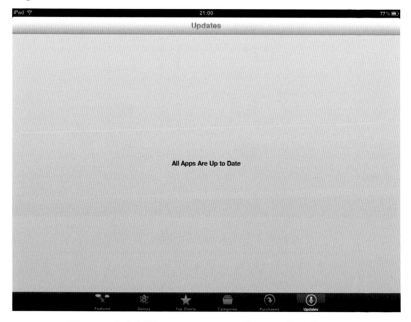

Figure 9-10 No apps currently need updating

iPhone Apps on the iPad

Your iPad will not only run apps designed for the iPad, but it can also run apps designed for the iPhone.

Just choose an app and install it as before then start using it, as shown in Figure 9-11.

These iPhone apps will not display in full screen mode as they are designed for much smaller screens. There is usually a 2x button in the corner to expand the screen but that usually results in a loss of quality.

Figure 9-11 iPhone apps on the iPad

Removing an App

At some point you will want to remove an app from your iPad. This might be because you have no further need for it, or because you want to reclaim some space (don't forget that every app you install uses precious space).

Fortunately it is very simple to remove an app. Just do the following:

1. Find the screen that has the app or apps you want to remove.

2. Press and hold any app on the screen until the apps start wobbling and a little X appears in the top left corner of each app, as shown in Figure 9-12.

Figure 9-12 Removing an app

3. Tap the X on the corner of the app you want to remove.

> Not all apps can be removed. You will notice certain apps don't have an X – they are the inbuilt system apps and as they are part of the iPad 2 OS they have to stay.

4. You will be asked to confirm you want to delete the app, as shown in Figure 9-13. Tap on Delete if you are sure.

Figure 9-13 Confirming you want to delete the app

> Don't worry if you change your mind after deleting an app, you can easily reinstall it whenever you like.

5. When you have removed all the apps you no longer want, just press the Home button and the apps will stop wobbling!

Getting Apps with iTunes

You can also choose and download apps from within iTunes. Sometimes this is easier to use if you are not sure what you are looking for and you just want to see things on a bigger screen.

So, to use iTunes to get apps:

1. Launch iTunes on your computer.

2. Click on the iTunes Store button to launch the store.

3. Click on the iPad button, as shown in Figure 9-14 (or if you want to find an iPhone app, just click on the iPhone button).

Figure 9-14 Looking for iPad apps in iTunes

4. Search for and select any apps that you are interested in getting for your iPad.

5. Once they have downloaded to your computer, just connect up your iPad and let the apps sync. They should then appear on your iPad ready to use.

Summary

In this chapter you have learnt about the App Store and how to select and install apps. You have also learnt how easy it is to remove an app when you are finished with it and how to use iTunes to get apps.

10

Other iPad 2 Apps and Features

So far we have looked at a number of the apps and features that come built in to your iPad 2, but there are quite a few more. In this chapter we will take a brief look at some of the other useful and interesting apps – but remember this is just the tip of the iceberg, so go and explore for yourself.

Listening to Music

You can use your iPad 2 to listen to music, as though it was a big iPod. In fact, the app you use to listen to music is called iPod. You can play some music via the iPod app whilst you do other tasks, such as checking your email or surfing the Internet.

To listen to music, do the following:

> Make sure you have music stored on your iPad – go back to Chapter 6 for more information.

1. From the Home screen, tap on iPod, as shown in Figure 10-1.

Figure 10-1 The iPod app

2. Your music library will now be displayed, as shown in Figure 10-2. Tap on any album to choose some music.

Figure 10-2 Your music library

You can change the views between Songs, Artists, Albums, Genres and Composers. Pick the view that you are most comfortable with.

3. From the list of available songs, as shown in Figure 10-3, tap on a song you want to listen to.

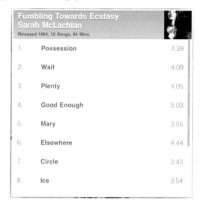

Figure 10-3 Picking a song to listen to

4. The song will now start playing. You can use the on-screen controls, as shown in Figure 10-4 to control the volume, pause the song, skip forward, back, etc.

Figure 10-4 On screen music controls

Looking at Photos

You can view photos on your iPad 2 and use it as though it was an electronic photo album. You can even view your photos as a slideshow while listening to music.

> Make sure you have photos stored on your iPad
> – go back to Chapter 6 for more information.

To start viewing photos, do the following:

1. From the Home screen, tap on Photos, as shown in Figure 10-5.

Figure 10-5 The Photos app

2. Your photos will then be displayed, as shown in Figure 10-6. Tap on any photo to display it full screen.

Figure 10-6 Your photos

3. Use your finger to swipe left and right between the photos.

> If you double-tap the screen, the area you tapped will be zoomed into. Double-tap again and it will zoom back out to normal size.

4. Tap the top of the screen and then tap Photos to go back to the photos display.

5. If you want to view your photos in a slideshow, just tap the Slideshow button to display the options shown in Figure 10-7.

Figure 10-7 Slideshow Options

6. You can select the types of transitions you want between the photos, if you want to listen to music, and if so, what music to listen to. When you have made your selection just tap Start Slideshow and sit back and enjoy the show.

7. You can stop the slideshow at any time by tapping the top of the screen.

> You can even start a slideshow from the lock
> screen by tapping the icon of a flower next to
> the slide to unlock button.

Making Video Calls with FaceTime

You can make video calls with your iPad 2 using the built-in
app called FaceTime. This enables you to connect with any
other FaceTime user (anyone with another iPad 2 or iPhone 4)
and enjoy high quality video calls.

> Unfortunately you cannot use FaceTime to
> make video calls with non FaceTime users.

To set up FaceTime for the first time, do the following:

1. From the Home screen, tap on the FaceTime app, as
   shown in Figure 10-8.

Figure 10-8 FaceTime

2. You will be asked to sign in with your Apple ID, as
   shown in Figure 10-9. Enter your details and tap Sign
   in to continue.

Figure 10-9 Signing into FaceTime

3. Follow through any additional questions that may be asked.

The next thing you need to do is add some contacts (if you don't already have contact details entered on your iPad):

1. Tap on the + button as shown in Figure 10-10.

Figure 10-10 Adding a contact

2. Enter in the contact details, as shown in Figure 10-11. You will need to enter in a name and either the phone number or email address of the contact and tap Done.

> If you want to use FaceTime to connect with an iPad 2 user then you only need the email address. If you want to connect to an iPhone 4 user you will need to enter their phone number.

Figure 10-11 Completing the contact details

Now if someone tries to contact you via FaceTime, you will immediately see a similar screen to the one shown in Figure 10-12. You can then tap Accept to start or Decline to ignore.

Figure 10-12 Someone is calling you

When you are taking part in a FaceTime call, you will see the main part of the screen, as shown in Figure 10-13, is that of the opposite party. What you are sending to them is shown in a smaller window in the bottom right corner.

Figure 10-13 A FaceTime call

If you want to change which camera you are using from the front to the rear, just tap the Camera swap button on the screen.

To initiate a FaceTime call from your iPad 2:

1. Tap on the contact you want to connect with.

2. Tap on either their email address or phone number to initiate the call.

Using the Camera on your iPad 2

Your iPad 2 has two cameras – one on the front and one on the rear. Both of the cameras can be used to take still pictures or to record video. The camera on the rear is the best one to use for video as it is higher quality.

> If you want to use the rear camera, make sure you don't cover the camera lens with your hand or your finger. Because of the placement of this camera it is really easy to do!

To start taking pictures with your iPad 2:

1. Tap on the Camera app from the Home screen, as shown in Figure10-14.

Figure 10-14 The Camera app

2. The image that can be seen through the camera lens will then be displayed, as shown in Figure 10-15.

> You can easily switch between the front and rear camera by tapping on the camera flip button.

Figure 10-15 The view through the camera

3. To take a picture, just tap the camera button in the centre of the bottom bar.

4. If you want to record video instead of still pictures, just slide your finger along the camera/video button as shown in Figure 10-16 until it selects video.

Figure 10-16 Selecting video

5. When you are ready to start recording video, tap the record button, as shown in Figure 10-17.

Figure 10-17 The video record button

6. To stop recording just tap the record button again.

> Your pictures and videos will appear in the Photos app. Don't try looking for your videos in the Videos app as this is purely for videos downloaded via iTunes.

Reading Books with iBooks

If you enjoy reading books, then an app you should get (which in my opinion should be part of the default apps) is iBooks. This can be downloaded for free via iTunes and enables you to download a huge library of free and paid for books which you can read on your iPad.

Figure 10-18 shows the books in your library:

Figure 10-18 Books in your library

You turn the pages of the book using your finger and it is surprising just how quickly you get used to reading this way.

Figure 10-19 shows an example of one of the many books you can download and read.

Figure 10-19 Reading a book on the iPad

Why not give it a try today?

Maps

Another useful app is Maps. Using the Maps app enables you to find exactly where you are, or search for a location, or even get directions from one place to another, all at the tap of the screen.

You can also choose between a classic map, a satellite image, a hybrid map or a terrain map. Figure 10-20 shows an image using the classic map.

Figure 10-20 Maps on your iPad

This uses the Google Maps software, so if you are familiar with this, it acts exactly the same. You can also zoom in to a very fine level of detail on a specific location. Why not take a look at your house – everyone does!

Summary

In this chapter you have learnt about a number of the other apps that come with your iPad 2, including ones that let you listen to music and view your photos. You have also learnt how to make video calls using FaceTime and how to get and read books using iBooks.

11

Troubleshooting

There isn't really much that goes wrong with the iPad 2, but every now and again something will go wrong.

The majority of times when something goes wrong, just simply switching the iPad off and then back on again will probably fix it. I know it is a bit of a cliché, but it does work!

Sometimes you may not be able to switch it off or close an app, and then more drastic measures are called for, in the form of a reset. Resetting your iPad forces the iPad to shut down and restart no matter what the problem is.

To perform a reset:

1. Press and hold the sleep / wake button.

2. Press and hold the Home button.

3. When the Apple logo appears on the screen let go of both buttons and wait until the iPad restarts.

Another thing that may cause you grief is if the battery completely runs out, there needs to be a little bit of a charge before iTunes will let you do anything. Just plug in your iPad and let it charge for a while before attempting to use it.

The most likely problems you will encounter will be to do with apps. Either the app won't run, or it keeps crashing. If that is the case you should remove the app and reinstall it. This also ensures that you are running the very latest version of the app.

Always try to ensure that you are running the very latest version of the iOS. Often there are bug fixes included which may resolve the problem you are experiencing.

> Remember that if all else fails, you can always perform a factory reset of your iPad 2. It is then up to you if you want to recover the last backup or start with a clean iPad.

Summary

In this very brief chapter you have learnt about some troubleshooting techniques. And now we have reached the end of the book. Good luck on your journey with your iPad 2.

Index